MASTERS IN ART

EL GRECO

Distributed in the U. S. A. and Canada
by
CROWN PUBLISHERS
419 FOURTH AVENUE NEW YORK, N. Y.

THE VIRGIN WITH SANTA INES AND SANTA TECLA
National Gallery, Washington. Widener Coll. detail

HYPERION MINIATURES

Theotocopuli

EL GRECO

BY

HENRI DUMONT

THE HYPERION PRESS

New York . Paris . London

FAMILY OF EL GRECO
Collection Theodore Pitcairn, Bryn Athyn, Pa.

EL GRECO

AN independent offshoot of the Italian Renaissance, nurtured on Spanish soil, Domenico Theotocopuli, the Greek, stands out not only as the link tween the art of Byzantium and that of Western Europe, but also, strange-enough, between the sixteenth century painters and the pioneers of modern t, Cézanne and the expressionists who followed in his wake.

The place of Greco's birth is but a conjecture and the exact date is un-own. It is thought that he was born in 1541, in the little village of odele near Candia in the isle of Crete. Nothing is known of his family, r of his early years. This much is certain: he helped to paint ikons, a lective, anonymous task in which the painter's individuality is lost in the quirements of tradition. When he was about twenty, possessed with the ge to study art and paint, he made his way to Venice, where he worked der no less a master than Titian.

[5]

In Venice, where Domenico was called "Il Greco," he met the m[ost] famous painters of the day, Veronese, Tintoretto and Jacopo di Bassa[no.] The latter took a particular fancy to the young man and their mutual [in]fluence has been the subject of many a controversy, several of Domenic[o's] earlier works having been attributed to Bassano, while in return, the Gr[eco] with his elongated figures and his very peculiar use of cold, bluish ti[nts] influenced to a certain extent the Italian master's style. However, it is Ti[nt]oretto's powerful dramatic art and Corregio's silvery colors that are echo[ed] in Domenico's Italian period, of which *The Lady in the Fur Cloak* and [the] *Portrait of Giulio Clovio,* the later painted in Rome, are the most outsta[nd]ing works.

In 1570, Domenico left Venice and travelled to Rome, on his way st[op]ping at Assisi where he saw the frescoes of Cimabue, the great Primit[ive] whose rendering of the life of St. Francis is in the tradition of Byzant[ine] ikon painting.

In Rome "Il Greco" was sponsored by Clovio, a miniature painter wh[ose] friendship with Cardinal Alessandro Farnese smoothed out Domenico's p[ath] in the capital. He remained there for two years and acquired considera[ble] repute. The period was one of clerical reaction against the pagan splend[or] of the Renaissance and Pope Pius V having commissioned painters to clo[the] the nude figures of Michael Angelo's *Last Judgment,* Domenico prou[dly] announced that he was prepared to paint another fresco in place of Mich[ael] Angelo's, which might as well be destroyed altogether. So much self-ass[ur]ance from a young artist and a newcomer to boot was not to be borne a[nd] it is said that Domenico left Italy because the indignation of his pe[ers] obliged him to seek his livelihood elsewhere.

It is not known why he chose Spain and Toledo in particular, b[ut] apparently the counter-reform instituted by the Jesuits appealed to [his] somewhat fanatical nature and moreover the decoration of the Escor[ial] attracted painters of renown from all over Italy. Domenico spent five yea[rs] at the Escorial and probably in Madrid as well. His Italian surname was [so] well-known by that time that it was left unchanged and only preceded [by] the Spanish "El."

In 1577, El Greco settled down in Toledo where the following year [his] son Jorge Manuel, was born to him. Art historians and novelists alike a[re] intrigued by Greco's life-long romance with the boy's mother, Doña Jeróni[ma] de las Cuebas, whose pensive features are reproduced in most of Domenic[o's] paintings, beginning with *The Lady in the Fur Cloak,* which seems to sh[ow] that he met her while yet in Venice. Was he married to her or not, and [if] so, when and where, and if not, why? This question has filled many [a] learned paragraph.

[6]

SAINT MARTIN AND THE BEGGAR
National Gallery of Art Washington, D.C. Mellon Coll. [7]

PORTRAIT OF AN OLD MAN
Collection F. H. Hirschland, New York

PORTRAIT OF EL GRECO
The Metropolitan Museum of Art, New York   [9]

The turning-point of Greco's art, the painting in which he first expres himself in his own manner, free from Italian suavity and full of the tra realism rooted in his Byzantine origin, was the *Espolio* painted sho after his arrival in Toledo, for the high altar of the cathedral. Altho greatly disconcerted by the unorthodox treatment of the subject, the chap accepted the picture but refused to pay the stipulated sum. Greco sued chapter and such was his prestige that he won his suit and acquired a grea authority than ever. He was again called to the Escorial by the King wh he painted the *Glory of Philip II* and the *Martyrdom of St. Maurice and Companions,* in both of which pictures, but particularly in the latter, he g full rein to his originality.

His cold, sinister oppositions of green and blue, and the use of grey which he was the first to see infinite possibilities of expression, had greatest influence on the Spanish school of which he was the unconsci founder.

At Toledo, Greco lived in a lordly fashion, scandalizing some a exciting the envy of all by his magnificence. Music inspired him and had musicians play to him during his meals. He set great store by his o works and would not part with any of them for less than the highest su that could be paid. In Spain at that time, artists were exempt from all tax so it is no wonder that Greco's fortune grew with the years.

One of the best known of his works, in which Domenico attains summit of his art, is the *Burial of the Count of Orgaz,* painted for the Cha of the Immaculate Conception at Santo Tomé. The Count, Don Gonzalo R de Toledo, was said to be a descendant of the Emperor of Constantino and the miracle which Greco represented was his entombment by St. Steph and St. Augustine descended from heaven in the presence of the large cro of mourners. Among these Greco depicted many well-known contemporar and the interest aroused by this painting was so great that people travell from afar to admire it.

The major art of Greco's works consists of purely religious paintings which the influence of Byzantium predominates over that of the Itali masters. The elongated figures and the upward movement of the compositi are strikingly his own, and far from being, as is believed by some, the res of astigmatism, they are a carefully calculated effect, designed to arouse t appropriate feeling of exaltation.

In the wake of St. Theresa of Avila, Greco was the first Spanish pain to depict and glorify St. Joseph who had hitherto been somewhat neglect by both artists and saints. Domenico also depicted St. Ildefonso, one Toledo's patron saints, in two importants works. *The Vision of St. Ildefon* in particular radiates with a serene and tender worship such as is seldo

[10]

THE RESURRECTION Prado, Madrid [11]

seen. For most of his saints, and he painted many of them—St. Hieronymu
St. Martin, St. Peter and St. Paul, to name only a few— his models wer
the Jews of the Toledan Jewish quarter where he lived: bearded old me
whose features the artist endowed with their natural fervor. In order t
have a true perspective when painting his compositions, he often used sma
clay or waxen figures which he sculptured himself and arranged in variou
effects of light and shadow. He loved the city of Toledo and depicted it i
several paintings, true to scale but with a facade changed according to h
whim.

His was a many-sided genius. Besides being a sculptor he was also a
architect and, according to his contemporaries, wrote numerous treatises nc
only on the arts but also on philosophy. No trace of his writings has, how
ever, been found.

Neither do we know of a specified portrait of El Greco, who was prou
but not vain of himself. However he is thought to have represented his ow
features in several compositions and nameless portraits which all concu
and resemble his *St. Luke* who, as the patron saint of painters, was tradition
ally depicted by most artists in their own image.

During the last years of his life, Greco acquired the reputation of
madman. He lived in a large house full of original copies of his own picture
but reduced in size. Absorbed in his painting he became more and more dar
ing in color and perspective. He had few friends, but among these were th
poet Gongora and Juan Pacheco, an indifferent painter who had the goo
fortune of listening to Greco's views on art, and then passing them on to h
son-in-law, Velázquez.

Thus we know that Greco placed color above drawing. He drew directi
with the brush instead of filling outlines with color, and his concern wa
chiefly with planes and the volumes these planes define. Centuries late
Cézanne was to rediscover the Spanish master's technique and in the bright
ness of Impressionism and outdoor painting make it wholly his own.

Domenico Theotocopuli died on April 7th, 1614, leaving a very com
plete will and bequeathing his estate, including two hundred and forty on
paintings, to his son Jorge Manuel, an architect and a painter of some repute
Mystery surrounds the final resting place of Greco for his ashes were trans
ferred from Santo Domingo el Antiguo to San Torcuato where his belove
Doña Jerónima joined him. This church was destroyed and the ashes of E
Greco disappeared.

Mysterious and impenetrable in private life, Domenico Theotocopul
the forerunner of modern painting, left many a mystery behind him fo
future generations to solve.

HENRI DUMONT

[12]

DETAIL OF THE HOLY FAMILY WITH
BOWL OF FRUIT   [13]

CHRIST OF THE MOUNT OF OLIVES
Collection Count A. Contini Bonacossi, Florence

BURIAL OF COUNT ORGAZ Church of Santo Tome, Toledo [15]

[16]   BURIAL OF COUNT ORGAZ Detail

BURIAL OF COUNT ORGAZ Detail   [17]

BURIAL OF COUNT ORGAZ Detail

DETAIL OF BURIAL OF COUNT ORGAZ   [19]

[20] THE ANNUNCIATION Collection Ralph M. Coe, Cleveland.

ST. ANNE, THE VIRGIN, THE INFANT CHRIST
WITH ST. JOHN Museum of San Vicente, Toledo   [21]

PORTRAIT OF LUIS DE GONZAGA
Bachstitz Gallery, The Hague

PORTRAIT OF THE ARCHITECT DON ANTONIO COVARRUBIAS
Museum of El Greco, Toledo   [23]

ST. FRANCIS IN MEDITATION
National Gallery of Canada, Ottawa

ST. FRANCIS IN MEDITATION detail [25]

THE VISITATION Library and Collection
Harvard University

PORTRAIT OF A YOUNG WOMAN WITH A FUR
Collection Sir John Stirling-Maxwell, Pollok House, Glasgow   [27]

CHRIST BEARING THE CROSS

Courtesy Tomas Harris, Ltd., London

THE VIRGIN Courtesy Strasbourg Museum [29]

[30]   CHRIST BEARING THE CROSS Art Gallery, Athens

THE ESPALIO Old Pinakothek, Munich   [31]

ST. JOHN THE BAPTIST AND ST. JOHN THE EVANGEL

[32]   Hospital of S. Juan Bautista, Toledo

ST. PHILIP Museum of El Greco, Toledo [33]

PORTRAIT OF GIULIO CLOVIO, THE MINIATURE PAINTER
Collection Count A. Contini Bonacossi, Florence.

ST. JOHN THE EVANGELIST
Museum of El Greco, Toledo

[36]

THE PENITENT ST. PETER
Fine Art Gallery of San Diego

[37]

[38] ST. LUKE Courtesy The Hispanic Society of America, New York

ST. JEROME Copyright The Frick Collection, New York [39]

[40]   ST. JAMES THE LESS Museum of El Greco, Toledo

ST. SIMON Museum of El Greco, Toledo [41]

[42]   THE VIRGIN detail Private Collection, London

ST. FRANCIS IN ECSTASY Detroit Institute of Arts [43]

ST. JEROME PENITENT National Gallery
of Scotland, Edinburgh

ST. PAUL detail Museum of El Greco, Toledo [45]

[46]   ST. ANDREW Museum of El Greco, Toledo

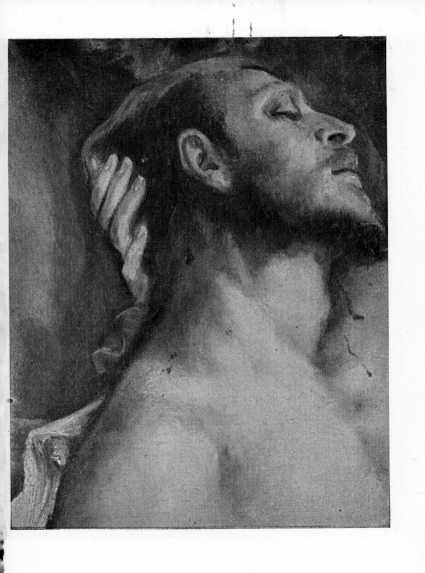

PIETA detail Collection Comtesse De La Beraudière, Paris [47]

THE
HYPERION MINIATURES
IN THE
MASTERS IN ART Series

present a new library, covering in individual volumes the life and art of all the great masters.

VAN GOGH • EL GRECO • DEGAS
RENOIR • BOTTICELLI • REMBRANDT
GOYA • CEZANNE

Each book is a complete Monograph with eight reproductions in full color and forty halftones.

In preparation:

MANET • GAUGUIN • TOULOUSE-LAUTREC
PICASSO • FRA ANGELICO
LEONARDO DA VINCI • BRUEGHEL
VELASQUEZ